George Du Maurier

Society pictures

George Du Maurier

Society pictures

ISBN/EAN: 9783741191640

Manufactured in Europe, USA, Canada, Australia, Japa

Cover: Foto ©Suzi / pixelio.de

Manufactured and distributed by brebook publishing software
(www.brebook.com)

George Du Maurier

Society pictures

SOCIETY PICTURES

BY

GEORGE DuMAURIER.

SOCIETY PICTURES

—BY—

GEORGE DuMAURIER

author of "Trilby" and "Peter Ibbetson."

CHICAGO:
CHARLES H. SERGEL COMPANY
1895

No. 11 Sergel's International Library. March 1895.

Published monthly. Entered at Chicago Postoffice as second class matter

By Subscription $3.00 a year.

AFTERNOON TEA.

STORY OF A BASHFUL MAN, WHO HAS PRIVATELY TOLD AN AUTHORS STORY TO THE HOST, AND HAS BEEN REQUESTED BY HIM TO REPEAT IT ALOUD FOR THE BENEFIT OF THE COMPANY. WE HAVE TRIED TO DEPICT THE WRETCHED INDIVIDUAL AT THE PRECISE MOMENT WHEN, HAVING REACHED TO WHENCE THENCE TWO-THIRDS OF HIS ANECDOTE (WHICH IS RATHER LONG), HE SUDDENLY DISCOVERS, ALL OF A SUDDEN, THAT HE HAS COMPLETELY FORGOTTEN THE POINT.

ALARMING SCARCITY.

SCENE—Club Smoking Room.

First Young Swell. "AW'—GOING ANYWHERE?"

Second Ditto. "NO !—ASKED TO THE 'ROW' TO-NIGHT ! THE IDEA HAS COMPLETELY FLOORED ME !"

Third Ditto. "BY JOVE ! I'VE BEEN THINKING OF LETTING MYSELF OUT AT TEN POUNDS A NIGHT. A FELLOW MIGHT RECOUP"

1874.

ARRESTED OF THE HONEYMOON.

"Don't move, Darling!—I'm so comfortable, and your Head is so Soft!!"

A SPORTING PLANT.

1897.

A DIFFERENT THING.

Proposition. "Ullo, Bertie! Is that you! How are you, Old Fellow! How much better they manage these things in France, eh? So jolly for a Fellow to be able to bathe with his own Family, you know!" Captain Rapid (indignantly). "Haw—yes—er another Fellow's Family, you know."

THE WARNING OF THE HONEYMOON.

Angelina (suggesting an inclination to please). "How nice it would be if some friend were to come up; wouldn't it, Edwin?" *Edwin (after pausing reluctantly).* "Yes — I — or even more likely!"

1878.

PUBLICATION.

Owner (_enthusiastically_). "What lovely Booth your Partner's got, Mary!"

Mary (_demurely_). "Yes, unfortunately he misses at the Wrong End."

RIVALS IN SOCIAL CIRCLES.

DINING AT AMVARD GRANGE.

A CAPTAIN'S PROPOSAL.

Lady Helen. "WELL, HELEN, WHAT ARE THESE?"

Helen (who has married recently). "THE DECANTER STOPPERS, MY LADY. JUST AFTER THE GENTLEMEN LEFT THE DINING-ROOM TO JOIN THE LADIES, SIR GORDON ASKED ME OF THE DECANTER, AS USUAL, BUT HE FORGOT THE STOPPERS; SO I THOUGHT I'D

A SUBTLE DISTINCTION.

Jones (who is of an inquiring mind). "AIN'T YOU GETTING TIRED OF SEEING PEOPLE SAY, 'THAT IS THE BEAUTIFUL MISS BELLAIR!!'?"

Miss Bellair (a Professional Beauty). "OH, NO. I'M GETTING TIRED OF HEARING PEOPLE SAY, 'IS *THAT* THE BEAUTIFUL MISS BELLAIR?'"

A DISCUSSION ON WOMAN'S RIGHTS.

Algernon (to his Sister, his Cousins, and his Aunts). "My dear Creatures, if you want Equality among the Sexes, you must learn to be independent of Us, as we are of You. Now we Men live entirely to please ourselves first, and then each other; whereas you Women live entirely to please Us!"

CONVINCING.

Proud Mother. "Did you ever see her attempt to Laugh and Scamper as Dear Alderson, Jack!"

Uncle Jack (æt. thirty-five). "Oh, you needn't trouble about that, Maria. I was exactly his build at Eighteen!"

CRINOLINED ALICE CARDS

"WHAT! ALL THAT FOR GRANDPA?"   "NO, DARLING. IT'S FOR YOU."   OH! WHAT A LITTLE BIT!"

1862.

EMPLOYER AND UNGALLERIED CONGRESS

Father Fred (who has been told by his Wife to make himself agreeable). "UNGENEROUS ALSO, AIN'T IT. SIR PORTER! FACT IS, BY WITH
THOUGHT IT WOULD BE BETTER FOR US ASK ALL THE BOYS WHO'VE ASKED US, AND GET US TO NEXT RACE OVER, AND PAY THEM
OFF IN THAT WAY. YOU KNOW! AND ERE SIR, BY JOVE! AND THE BEST OF IT IS, THEY'VE ALL COME!!!!!"

THERE ONE WOULD WISH TO HAVE REMAINED CONTENTEDLY.

THINGS TO BE LIVED DOWN.

A TIMELY CAUTION

Jack. "You mustn't be so proud of your hair, Effie! Remember that we are mostly it might all be taken by the top of your head, and we'll all wear your fall like your Aunt Matilda's? Mustn't it, Aunt Matilda?"

A FAIR RETORT.

A FELT WANT.

Eligible Young Aspirant. "AND DO YOU REALLY APPROVE OF GLADSTONE FOR YOUR LEADER, MR. PRENDERGAST?"

Proud Mother. "I DO, INDEED, MR. MILDMAN, AND ALWAYS HAVE. I HAD ASKED YOU THAT THERE IS NOT ONE OF MY DAUGHTERS THAT COULDN'T KNOCK BOTH HIS EYES FATHER!"

CRAMMING IT.

"What? going already! And is Macintosh? Surely you are not going to Wait!"

"Oh, dear no! Lord Archibald is going to take us to it in a pair little Ship he's fitted out near the Midhouse—with a Pleasure place! Together from Things gleaned up Out Bill, and so Widdow home—and the Waterloobers are to help out Dinnertime, you know, and dine unto Diamond, and all that!"

THE MAIDEN'S POINT OF VIEW.

Mamma (to Maud, who has been with her Brother to the Play, and is full of it). "But was there no Love in the Piece, then?" Maud. "Love! Oh dear no, Mamma. How could there be? The principal Character was Husband and Wife, you know!"

PLEASANT!

Lord Reginald Gadabout (in answer to confidential remark of his Host). "TWENTY THOUSAND POUNDS' WORTH OF PLATE ON THE TABLE, SIR GORGIUS! I WONDER YOU AIN'T AFRAID OF THESE BUTLERS!"

Sir Gorgius Midas. "AFRAID, MY LORD! GOOD LOR! I'VE SEEN THE LOUMMIE'S NOT WORTHLESS ENUFF TO STEAL OF LATE."

AWKWARD CORNER. "THE CROWDED REGIONS OF THE STAGE."

Fond Mother. "PRAY SILENCE, GENTLEMEN, FOR SIR PORTLY BOODELL!"

Sir Portly Bobell. "HER GRACIOUS—AND—GRACIOUS——"

Cripsly (sotto to Peascombe de Tompkyns). "ANNE, A VERY FORCED DISTINCTION!"

59

FAME.

Son of the House (to the Hero of the Day). "ARE YOU ANY RELATION TO THE WILLIAMS?"

General Sir Archibald Williams, G.C.B., G.C.S.I., V.C., &c., &c., &c. "THE WILLIAMS?"

(The Question of an Hour before Dinner.)

THE CLOTHES SEASON.

(Mrs. Ponsonby de Tomkyns at Home—"Early and late.")

Mr. P. de T. (to the Waiter). "WOULD YOU MIND ONE OF YOU, DRIVE AS VERY FAST AS YOU TO GIVE ME THE LOAN OF A FOOL, OR SOMETHING. I'M—I'M MASTER OF THE HOUSE."

CUTTING.

Mama. "These obstinate French didn't seem to understand their own language, Amy!"

Amelia. "Not as you speak it, Love! By the way, I would recommend you always to speak French in France, when you have anything of a Confidential Nature to impart to be before the Natives! So easy of them understand a little English, you know!"

IT IS ALWAYS WELL TO BE WELL-INFORMED.

Sh. "Who's my Sister's Partner, Philippa, with the Star and Ribbon!"

Ph. "Oh, er—er—He's Sir—Sir—plase me, I forget his Name—but, you know, he went anywhere as others or others to look after that Scientific Fellow, who was his Name?—you know, who was Lost or something, or else Killed by somebody!"

"NONE BUT THE BRAVE, DESERVE THE FAIR!"

Lady Clara (who is rather timid, and wants to sit down). "IF YOU ARE REALLY SO DEVOTED AS YOU SAY YOU ARE, SIR CHARLES,

I'LL TELL YOU HOW YOU CAN SHOW YOUR DEVOTION."

Sir Charles (of the Grenadier Guards). "YES, BY—! OH, YES! BY—"

Lady Clara. "WELL—YOU CAN TAKE THAT DEAR OLD LADY DOWN TO SUPPER, YOU KNOW—AND THEN I CAN HAVE HER CHAIR!"

HAPPY THOUGHT.

UNDER PRETENCE OF THROWING A REFLECTED LIGHT ON THE FACE, THAT BRINGS YOUNG PORTRAIT PAINTER, FIMMM, ALWAYS PROVIDES HIS SITTER WITH SOMETHING SO PLEASANT TO LOOK AT, THAT HIS ONE NEVER GETS TIRED OF LITTLE (I.E. STANDING). THIS ALSO EXPLAINS WHY HIS PORTRAITS ALWAYS HAVE THAT SYMPATHETIC AND THOUGHTFUL, ELEGANCE OF CONTEMPLATIVE SERENITY.

THREE ONE WOULD RATHER HAVE LEFT UNPAID.

She. "Would you rather be sitting by Lake-Tahoe Shore on your Postcard, Mr. Green?"

He. "I'm afraid by Postcard and barely on dining, Miss Grand; but I shall be delighted to carry them for you!"

THE LAST BALL OF THE SEASON.

(Scene—Orwell Hotel, Lowestone—in zept. Nov.)

AROUND THE TEATABLE

(The Comforts of Culture at Home – Small and Early.)

Mrs. Mivens (indignantly, to her husband). "Look, Look! Mr. and Mrs. Stickleback, of all People! To think of their Stickleback being here!?"

Mr. Mivens. "Yes, Love! And to think of their being the only People in the Room we know!"

EXTREME DISTRESS.

The Mayor (to Nephew, who wants taking down a bit, à Binks). "WHAT! FOR REAL, PERCY! AIN'T YOU RATHER FOND OF AS GOING TO BALLS!"

Percy. "WHAT, AND YOU HEAR THE, UNCLE! WHY, I SHOULD HAVE THOUGHT YOU'D GIVEN UP THAT KIND OF THING LONG AGO!"

1884.

DISTINGUISHED AMATEURS.—THE BANJOIST.

"UNFISH AND FISH BY CANDIDATE!"—BYRON.

"DO YOU THINK HUSBAND TO SING, LAURA!"———"I WILL, IF YOU WILL PROMISE TO ASK HIM TO LEAVE OFF!"

THE POWER OF IMAGINATION.

Good Child (to Doctor, who has just been taking his temperature). "AH, SIR! *I FEAR* THERE BE A LOT O' COLD, SIR!"

SOCIAL AGONIES

Snob (whose sense of humour is quite abnormal). "OH, BY THE WAY, I SENT YOU A VERY NEAT ARTY SMITH—JUST A STIFF TRIPO!—TWO FLAYF!! YOU'LL ALL BE OF LEISURED WHEN I TELL YOU ...." [*Tells him. Nobody remembers but he*

THOSE ONE WOULD RATHER HAVE LEFT UNSAID.

She (to her Partner). "DO YOU LIKE THE LANCERS?"

TRUTHS THAT MIGHT HAVE BEEN LEFT UNSPOKEN.

Helen. "What! Haven't you brought the bottle, Mr. Jones!"

Mr. Jones. "No! You couldn't get Mrs. Smith. The fact is, they're giving presents for Mrs. Brown's Diary"

AN EYE FOR ESSENTIALS.

Mamma (House-hunting, for the Season). "It's a good House for a Dance, Emily!"

Emily. "The Rooms are rather small, aren't they!"

Mamma (who knows her Member so well). "Yes; but what a capital Staircase!"

"Look, Dear! There's your Richard going in to supper with Mrs. Somebody—a remarkably attractive woman. Let us go too!"

"How good of you! Now I was so was going in to supper with you, Dear, instead!"

"HERE'S A POST-OFFICE!" 1797. 1857.

(A Chapter on the Evolution of Departments.)

HAVING A GOOD TIME.

Mamma. "It's very late, Emily. Has Arthur taken you home to supper?"

Fair Débutante (who has a fine healthy appetite). "Oh yes, Mamma—several times!"

SOCIAL AGONIES.—THE RECITAL.

A CAUTION TO LADIES

(Drawn by their Treacherous Glass Fans.)

Sir Peppery Blankett. "WELL—A—NOW THAT I HAVE PROMPTORLY EXPLAINED TO YOU THAT MY CONVICTIONS ARE WITH REGARD TO THE [said QUESTION], I WILL PROCEED TO—— BUT—A—I AM REALLY ALMOST AFRAID I BEGIN TO PERCEIVE—A—THAT MY VIEWS OF THE SUBJECT FAIL TO AMUSE YOUR JUDGMENT, MADAM!"

THINGS ONE WOULD WISH TO HAVE EXPRESSED DIFFERENTLY.

Gust. "Well, Good-bye, Old Man!—and you've really got a very jolly little Place here!"

Host. "Yes; but it's awfully bare, just now. I hope the Trees will have Grown a good bit before you're back, Old Man!"

187.

THINGS ONE WOULD RATHER HAVE LEFT UNSAID.

Major le Maréchal. "How Charming [—a—so DELIGHTFULLY PLAYED [—a—such a LOVELY COUNTENANCE [—a—I ONLY HEARD 'EM LAST FEW BARS—a—BUT IT WAS QUITE ENOUGH!"

THERE ONE WOULD RATHER HAVE LEFT UNSAID.

She. "No! I can't give you another Dance. But I'll introduce you to the Prettiest Girl in the Room!"

_He._ "But I don't want to Dance with the Prettiest Girl in the Room. I want to Dance with you!"

Aunt Bess. "I wonder, James, at your encouraging young Caddy to be so rude with Madeline! He's a sad bore, and not a good friend, I fear!"

Papa. "Oppose him, no! I've given his grandfather to come when he likes, and he's getting rather tired of him at last, for I'm always calculating—"

AWKWARD REVELATIONS.

Edy. "Oodbody and I have been down-stairs in the Dining-room, Mr. Mitcham. We've been playing Horses and Wives!"

Mr. Mitcham. "How did you do that, my dear?"

Edy. "Why, Grimby sat at one end of the Table, and I lay at the other; and Grimby said, 'Two Pigs isn't my nay!' and I said, 'It's all you'll get!' and Grimby said, 'Dear!' and I got up and left the Room!"

FOND AND FOOLISH.

Edwin (suddenly, after a long pause). "DARLING!" *Angelina.* "YES, DARLING!"

Edwin. "NOTHING, DARLING. ONLY DARLING, DARLING!"

[*Believes Old Gentleman found out, etc.*]

THERE ONE WOULD RATHER HAVE LEFT UNSAID.

"OH, I AM SO PLEASED TO MAKE YOUR ACQUAINTANCE, MR. M'GINTIE! I HAVE HEARD OF YOU AND YOUR WORKS FOR EVER SO LONG—THE LAST TEN OR FIFTEEN YEARS, I AM SURE!"

NOBLE SELF-SACRIFICE IN THE CAUSE OF CHARITY.

The Duchess of Belgravia. "THAT'S MY CHAPTER FOR THE DANCE IN THE THIRD ACT—RATHER COLD IN THIS WEATHER—BUT IT'S FOR THE POOR CRIMPING-SHREDDERS' WIDOWS' HOME, YOU KNOW! ARE YOU COMING TO SEE IT, CAPTAIN DE BOOTS!" *Gallant Hussar.* "HAW! HAW! I SHOULD RATHER SAY SO, DUCHESS—RATHER! WOULDN'T MISS IT FOR THE WORLD! BRING THE

SOCIAL PROMENADE.

His Lordship (confidentially with the seat). "Brava! Bravissimo! Beautiful! Go on! I could listen all day!" (Aside to Footman.) "Just see if my Carriage is come. Look sharp!"

SPLICED TO BE LIVED DOWN, IF POSSIBLE.

Reggy. "I had hoped for the pleasure of taking you down to supper, Mr. Karan!"

Reggy. "Too late, my dear fellow! It's the early bird that catches the worm!"

A SOCIAL DILEMMA

Pah Vader, "There's that lovely Woman again. I wonder who she is!"

M. le Bebe (an experienced observer). "Papa, I tink she must be a English Duchess, because she in the party, she dress well, she speak more like Ros, and say, 'You bet,' and she talk about Dollars and Cars!"

Inquisitive Old Gentleman. "WHO'S WON!"   First Football Player. "WE'VE LOST!"
Inquisitive Old Gentleman. "WHAT HAVE YOU GOT IN THAT BAG!"   Second Football Player. "THE UMPIRE!"

FALSE MODESTY.

Fair Hostess (who is proud of her pianoforte). "Yes; I flatter myself there's not a Door-bell in the whole Street that's no other Sound as mine."

Fair Father. "Well, Dear, I had to Ring it Five Times!"

COACHED TO BE LIVED DOWN.

The New Servant. "Oh, so glad to see you, Mary! But we've such dreadful colds, we can't kiss you, dear. We can only shake hands!" *Fair Visitor.* "Oh dear, how sad! I sort for haven't got a cold, Mr. Brown!!"

KINDLY MEANT.

(Scene—A Dance at the Private Houses (his Madame Tussaud's).)

Ingenuous Hostess (to Arrived Chaperone). "AS—I SAY—AWFULLY DREADFUL HERE, DON'TCHERKNOW. WON'T YOU GO AND PUT UP IN THE 'CHAMBER OF HORRORS'—THEY'VE GOT A STOVE, AND YOU'LL FEEL SO MUCH MORE AT HOME THERE, DON'TCHERKNOW."

HARDLY COMPETENT.

Brown (to Smith). "Yes! There sits Jones, as usual, with a crowd of admiring disciples hanging on his lips, and compelling at his feet, and following him all over the room! How disgusting it is to see a man of genius toadyied."

1886.

A PRACTICAL REMINDER.

Sir Acres. "AND HAVE YOU TO ROME?" *American Lady.* "I GUESS NOT." (*To her Daughter.*) "SAY, BELLA, DID WE VISIT ROME?" *Fair Daughter.* "WHY, MA, CERTAINLY! DON'T YOU REMEMBER? IT WAS IN ROME WE BOUGHT THE LILAC-THREAD STOCKINGS!"

HAPPY THOUGHT.

"Oh, I say, Old Man, I wish you'd run upstairs and bring her down to supper. She's an Old Lady, is a Red Body, and a Green Skirt, and a Blue and Yellow Train, with an Orange Bird of Paradise in——"

REFLECTIONS OVERHEAD.

He. "BY THE BYE, TALKING OF OLD TIMES, DO YOU REMEMBER THAT OCCASION WHEN I MADE SUCH AN AWFUL ASS OF MYSELF."

She. "WHICH?"

THE ASTONA.

The Baron (to Mrs. Maudera, who is looking her very best). "Heavens, dear! I hope you're not as Thank as you look!"

(Assault of a Quiet Neighbourhood.)

THINGS ONE WOULD RATHER HAVE EXPRESSED DIFFERENTLY.

Jones (nervously conscious that he is entertaining a pleasant Maid élé). "A—I'D LIKE TO SAY I'D BEEN TOLD TO TAKE YOU IN TO SUPPER, MISS BROMMY!"

www.ingramcontent.com/pod-product-compliance
Lightning Source LLC
Chambersburg PA
CBHW030558270326
41927CB00007B/976